YOUR SH*TTY FAMILY

D0452010

YOUR SH*TTY FAMILY

PRESENTED BY UNSPIRATIONAL

Abrams Image, New York

Editor: Samantha Weiner
Designer: Devin Grosz
Production Manager: Alex Johnson
Illustrations: Heesang Lee

Library of Congress Control Number: 2017930313

ISBN: 978-1-4197-2419-0

ABRAMS The Art of Books
115 West 18th Street, New York, NY 10011
abramsbooks.com

CONTENTS

INTRODUCTION

There are moments in your life that you will never forget. I had one of those when I was seventeen. It was my sister's birthday and to celebrate we got her a carb-free cheesecake because she was in one of those phases in her life where she decided that carbs were the devil. We all took a bite of the cake and immediately knew that it belonged in the garbage. I'm not sure what came over me in that moment, but I took off my shirt and slammed my face into the cake—it was something I had always wanted to do. The carb-free cheesecake filling clumped in my goatee, and through my frosted eyelashes I could see the horrified face of my mother, who was watching as her child went completely wild. Again, I'm not sure what came over me, but I then grabbed the remaining cheesecake from the platter and rubbed it all over my chest and nipples. At this point our two Irish setters became very excited, as they detected there might be some errant cheesecake coming their way.

I, of course, seized the opportunity and ran through the living room, out the front door, and into the street in front of our house. My mother stood horrified in the doorway as her almost adult son, completely covered in garbage cheesecake, danced around in public, being chased by two ravenous adult dogs. It was a dance that drove her mad, and not in a good way. She ran to her room and closed the door behind her. Between the shitty cheesecake and her demented son, the celebration had been completely and totally ruined.

A few years later, my mother was diagnosed with cancer. It was the worst time in her life and, of course, the worst time in mine. But as we sat in the hospital room together, it was stories like this that made us laugh harder than anything else. These terrible moments, these pitiful displays of humanity, these lapses in judgment. These were the things that let us look back on our lives and know that no matter how much we got under each other's skin, we would always forgive each other. We may be shitty. But we're family.

She's better now, and now the stories of her horrible times in the hospital have somehow become funny, too. That's how life works. So, as you go through this book of painful, cringe-worthy, terrifying texts, remember that when you look back on the life you've lived, it won't just be the good moments you remember, it'll be the shitty ones, too. And those are the ones that are really going to make you laugh.

BAD DAD

When you are growing up, you think your dad has it all figured out. And then you get older and you realize he's just a big, dumb idiot.

DAD

I love you

Fuck you

Should have pulled out

I really do hate you

* It's your fault he's here, pal

PADRE   TODAY 4:16 PM

What we doing for dinner

I don't know I've been shitting for the past 30 minutes. My butthole hurts so bad

Good thing u don't eat with your ass

* Yes, it is a good thing not to eat with your ass

DAD   TODAY 12:37 PM

Good luck on your final see ya later

Thanks

If you don't ace it, don't bother coming home

oh thanks

* Motivation!

Happy birthday beautiful.
Xoxo.

Thanks Pa. And thanks
for creating me 👍

2 of the best minutes ever.

Ew.

Sorry.

* Too real

PAPA

drive slowly and safely, mum said she wanted another night of rampant sex 😜

Love you x

Lovely. I'll sleep in my car

* He may never come home again

PAPA TODAY 1:22 PM

Having a good head day today! 👍 👍 👍

There's nothing better than good head. hahaha, yeah I said it

DADDDDDD

* Is there a way to pretend this conversation never, ever, ever happened?

DADDIO MONDAY 10:11 AM

This hot chick next to me keeps hitting on me.

What should I do???

Hahahaha no she's not.

Leave her alone. She doesn't like you.

* ICE COLD

DAD JAN 4 7:13 PM

How long have your mother and I been married? Don't ask her or she'll get really mad. Just find out somehow!!!

* Covert Pops

DADDY TODAY 5:03 PM

Hi my love, I am losing my memory sorry!, could you pls tell me the birthdays of my sons and daughters? Thanks

Um... I'm an only child, aren't I?

* Maybe he could store this information somewhere? Like, in his phone?

DAD TODAY 8:07 PM

Happy Valentine's Day. 24 years ago today mom and I created you. I love you.

* V-O-M-I-T

Do u prefer smoked gammon?

To what?

I smoked

Are you high?

What are you on about dad?

Meat ford armies

Samies

WHAT IS GOING ON

All will be explained x

* High Dad is a very Cool Dad

Will you come get me?

omg 😜

Dad please, it's raining

omg 💁‍♀️

DAD

omg 🤷‍♀️

I'm going to tell mom

omg no 😔

* TEEN DAD!

DADDY   TODAY 11:11 AM

hey. I'm just about to give your MOM
the high hard one for Mothers day.
What do you want? Love you.

I'm gonna throw up.

* JESUS. CHRIST.

DAD   TODAY 2:12 PM

ugh this class is so easy I love it

That's not good news.

Why not?

Can't I love something that's easy

Well, I guess it's fine. I loved your mom

* Well played

DAD THURSDAY 7:47 PM

Call your mom she's hammered and funny

Hahahahha OK

* Some dads know how to have a good time

DAD TODAY 8:55 AM

Have you heard from mom?

I texted her last night at nine and this morning at 730 then just tryed calling her and went straight to voicemail. I'm sure she is ok just kinda concerned

She was on Facebook this morning around 6 am because she had liked stuff on my Facebook

???wtf???

* Mom is most definitely cheating

DADDY   TODAY 3:45 PM

Dinner at home?

Yes

Fish?

Yeesh

You like salmon

Don't tell me what I like

YOU LIKE SALMON

* HE RAISED YOU AND GODDAMN IT YOU LIKE SALMON

DAD   TODAY 11:03 AM

hey can u send me pic
of your 1099-T?? Thx

Yeah

Yea I'm doing my taxes and need those

Make her hubby finger your woman's ass

Um don't think that was
supposed to go to me

oh yeah oops LOL!

I do need the tax form soon :)

* Bleach my eyeballs

DAD FRIDAY 8:22 PM

Want me to tell you how we got you

Definitely no

Me and mom were in a melon patch on the side of the rode and we saw a baby and it said "I want a lollipop." So I knew you belonged with us and even though your mother wanted to take you to SPCA I told her no, we take the candy baby home

So I saved you.

* Dad loves mushrooms

DADDY BOB TODAY 6:40AM

Have a good day! don't ask me for money today

Impossible

* You can't ask her not to do what she was born to do

TODAY 8:27 AM

Happy Father's Day xxxx

Thanks, but I don't think that I am your father :(

.....

* We know whose paperweight is getting returned to SkyMall

DAD

MONDAY 10:27 AM

Hey—very important to check your tire pressure this week. When it gets cold. Pressure typically goes down.

Stay safe!

And I'm not talking about using a condom!

Oh my god, please go away

* Thanks for the mental image

This is your father.

You are adopted.

* Cool. So I guess there's no need to respond then

DAD THURSDAY 10:16 AM

I had just masturbated in the waiting room

Lmao that was for mom

I'm at the doctors office and she can't believe I have low blood pressure

HAHAHAHAH omfg that's so funny. I just actually laughed out loud.

She said I must be drunk and that was my answer

I was like wow dad. It's cool and all that ur comfortable with me but...

Lmao

* And why would Mom want that information anyway?

DAD YESTERDAY 4:30 PM

Odd question of a father to his daughter but, do you have my dummy hand grenade?

It's missing

* She put it in the attic with all your other fake explosives, you weirdo

DAD TUESDAY 9:14PM

Can I take the truck tomorrow?

Who dis

Your daughter....

Oh, hi julia.

No.

* New dad. Who dis?

DAD THURSDAY 2:51 PM

Stop being a bitch
I hate u

That was your sister

I figured

Sorry... Damn kids.

* It's always the "sister"

DAD FEB 25 8:29 AM

Thank you, Kim

This is Alison. Love u still :)

Sorry, me bad

* Yes. You bad

YESTERDAY 12:58 PM

Why are you only friends with me on Facebook?

That's all I wanted it for.

Creeper

;)

TODAY 5:08 PM

Hey I will creep you later

Pardon?

I will check out your facebook

That's great dad

* Blocked. Blocked. BLOCKED!

So how's the blizzard going?

Bitch.

* Vacation is better when others are suffering

POPPY TUESDAY 6:04 PM

No matter what do not let any guy strangle you during sex. They just found another American girl dead in her apartment in Italy from this. Look up Amanda Knox on the Internet. Same thing happened with her.

LOL I don't think you have to worry about that dad

* She uses safe words, Dad

DAD TUESDAY 5:17 PM

Wifi password not working.
They may have changed it.

Maybe you're typing it in without proper capital letters or something

Listen Einstein. It's all numbers so no caps issue. U best check urself.

* Before you wreck yourself

My car won't start

Why not you just need a new battery

The elbow fell off the overflow pipe
and I was trying to get it back on and
my phone fell out of my pocket

I put it in rice and it's working

Try putting your car in rice

lol

* Thanks for all your help, Dad

PAPA FRANK MAR 17 9:35 AM

Blake Lively is pregnant.
how upset are you?

It is my child
Do not be upset
A new sibling

* Delusional Dad™

DAD TODAY 9:22 AM

House still there?

Nah burnt it down sorry

Get laid?

Oh yeah 😳

Good thing one of us is getting some

* The house was a small price to pay

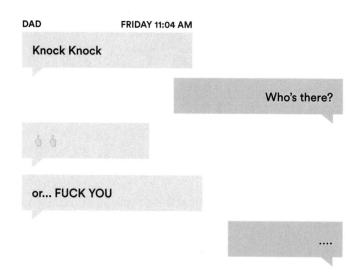

DAD   FRIDAY 11:04 AM

Knock Knock

Who's there?

or... FUCK YOU

....

* When you eat all the ice cream in the freezer and don't tell anyone

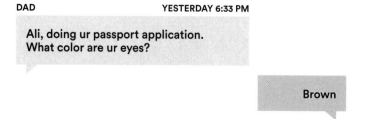

DAD   YESTERDAY 6:33 PM

Ali, doing ur passport application.
What color are ur eyes?

Brown

* You really should know this in case she ever gets kidnapped

SUNDAY 4:11 PM

We went to the zoo

Nice!

Why is your mother at the zoo?

* She's looking for bigger bananas, Dad!

DAD   **FRIDAY 12:02 PM**

how's school going

is your middle name
Ann or Anne

> Ann. School is going well

* Weren't you a part of that decision?

DAD   **JAN 21 5:51 PM**

What are you up to?

> It's snowing out. It's so cold! I'm
> making chili tho so we're all good

Netflix and chili?

> omg do you know what that phrase means? 🛡

* Netflix and chili is pretty clever, though . . .

Using your visa for porn is the fastest way to lose everything

What are you talking about??

I didn't

You made a purchase for $28.89 porn web site

I made a purchase for 28.89 to the couch tomato. It's a pizza place

I was wrong I googled the name and a bunch of porn came up

That's a weird sounding porn

* Nothing turns me on like a couch tomato

POPS TODAY 8:04 AM

How was softball?

> Went really good. I played 3rd and hit pretty well. hand is pretty sore this morning. Felt good hearing the other team say "do not hit it to third base!!!!"

I remember your little league coach telling his team the same. I was concerned for your pussy hands! 😒

TODAY 10:22 AM

> LOL!

Don't blame me. You got your pussy hands from your mom.

* Pussy hands?

Are you coming home anytime soon???

Maybe

Please come home! 😭 😭 there's a bug on the microwave it's a roach and I need to heat up my coffee and I'm crying. This thing is being all shifty and climbing in and out of the vent and I'm just not ok.

thank you that cheered me up a little

* Glad you enjoy her misery SO MUCH

DAD   **THURSDAY 11:30 AM**

Hi Jaclyn. I hope you're having a good day. I noticed that you got poop all over the bottom of the toilet seat downstairs.

Please clean that up. Thank you.

* But once upon a time, he used to clean her ass!

POPS   APR 18 5:27 PM

Is mom okay? I've texted her five different days and she doesn't reply to me. But I know she always has her phone and iPad attached to her hip.

She doesn't like you any more.

That's what I figured. Oh well!

* Sometimes your parents just fall out of love with you

THE MOMSTER UNDER MY BED

She brought you into this world, but sometimes the things she says make you wish you were never born.

MOM

What is Glory Hole and Pixilated bukkake?

Mom, no.

DO NOT GOOGLE THAT

* STEP AWAY FROM THE COMPUTER!

MOMS   YESTERDAY 8:52 PM

Well what did she write

She just wrote "lmfao"

She does have a
fat ass and mouth

F stands for fucking mom. not fat 😂

Oh
I'm dumb

* From now on it should mean Laughing My Fat Ass Off

MOMMY   AUG 30 7:36 PM

I saw a bee poop today

🐝. 💩

* Nature is magical

Hey. How are you?

Hot sluts

I am a human fucking walking corn

I miss your FAE

I used to hang out of a bath with a dog

Ugly baby gatorade insurance

Ring a fucking pizza

Nice bra

I stutter

* They let you make a human?

MOMMY **TODAY 11:10 AM**

Your an amazing daughter.

* You're

MOMMA HELEN **YESTERDAY 8:11 PM**

Ok what if someone asked you to "come and chill and watch Netflix". How would you interpret this?

YESTERDAY 9:19 PM

Mom it means they wanna hit it

I'm so out of it!!!

Was told that but needed to confirm lol

Netflix and chill is code for the booty

Who asked you

* The thought of Mom hooking up gives me the Netflix and chills

MOM

Call me back ya weirdo

SUNDAY 12:19 PM

Call me back mom

TODAY 7:58 AM

Out with my boyfriend. Don't want him to know I have kids.

* Seems like a great way to meet your new father . . .

MAMA YESTERDAY 1:55 PM

How everyone's day going?

YESTERDAY 4:40 PM

Did u see above?

YESTERDAY 5:44 PM

Yes, everything is fine

Ok

TODAY 8:22 AM

Starting to walk waking up.
He slept really late

TODAY 9:26 AM

He wants cars again!

TODAY 11:24 AM

Thinking about lunch, do you want him
to have the flour or corn taco shells?
And is your text working today?

* She thinks it's a group text, but it's not

hey what are we having for supper

your skank ass thighs if you don't get your ass down here to do the dishes

* OK, but what's for dessert?

MOM   YESTERDAY 12:18 AM

We ran the batteries down on all our phones and had only one car charger. Guess what we are doing tomorrow?

Sleeping in?

Probably about 8

Ok so what are you really doing?

Nothing that we can talk with our kids about!
😂 😂

* Grooooooosssssssss

MOM YESTERDAY 7:13 PM

Get your mother some cheap vodka and orange juice, will ya?

I'm only 20 but

Oh fuck. Damnit.

I keep forgetting

* How do you not remember when you gave birth to a human?

MOM SATURDAY 2:42 PM

Your an amazing mom

*You're

Haha see!

* When your kid is nice but also an idiot

MA   THURSDAY 9:46 PM

Cannot believe that u r sleeping

U better call me back

THURSDAY 10:22 PM

What r u doing?

Hello!!!!

THURSDAY 11:56 PM

R u mad at me for calling u later?

Don't be a Virgo

If I don't talk to u, I'm going
to be worried all night

* Mom, you're acting like a real Pisces

BIRTH GIVER   JAN 18 6:22 PM

Thanks for not getting pregnant

or doing drugs

Mom, I'm pregnant and on coke

No, you're full figured and that's sprite

* It's all fun and games until someone says what they're thinking

MOM   **TODAY 10:34 AM**

Dont forget to water flowers in the am when its this hot not during mid day

TODAY 4:26 PM

Remember I'm too young to be a grandma and paid too much for your education so be careful

Also when you grill use low so it won't catch fire love you

* This is a lot of Mom all at once

MOMMY   **MAR 19 5:04 PM**

Maybe you should just skip the movie tonight and just let Ryan come over and walk your weiner...

He'd probably prefer it the other way around

* Is Mom suggesting the elusive reverse hand job?

MOM   TUESDAY 11:56 PM

Hewwwwoooooooo   It's me

I was wondering if after all of
these minutes you'd like to call

To go over everything

They say match.com can work to heal ya

But if you don't call I won't
do much healing . . .

Hewwwwoooooooo

Ok now let me know you're alive please

YESTERDAY 1:51 AM

Helllooooook

I'm cal8ing the police if u don't text me

* This kind of behavior deserves to be ignored . . .

MOM   YESTERDAY 7:45 PM

I saw a new show on tv that
reminded me of you.

What was it

Bad Kids Go To Hell

:/

* All dogs go to heaven, but you won't be there

MOMMA   FRIDAY 9:21 AM

Thanks for setting the A/C
to 70 before you left!

My ass is frozen

Good, wake your ass up
and heat it up

* Save money by freezing your child to death

MUMMA MAY 10 9:12 PM

COCONUT OIL
TRY IT

I'm your mother, I know this stuff
It's great for anal 😉

Goodbye!

* How to ruin coconut oil forever

MA YESTERDAY 9:27 PM

Yeah John said he wanted my blessing

Did you give it to him?

I said show me your bank account first

I love you

* Priorities!

What's the number for uber

🙄 It's an app you download your phone

OK can u download it for me

No . . . you have to do it on your phone

I'll invite you. Hold on

Hold on to what

* 1-800-FUCK-U-MOM

MOTHERSHIP

Stop using my razor

You used a lot of my things
for 9 months without asking,
and besides half of that hair on
your legs is my DNA anyway

* OK, but to be honest she never asked to live in your uterus

Is that dad dog mushing naked on Facebook?

* Please don't talk to your kid about your fetishes

I don't care if your jeans are ripped, I am not coming to get you now. You still have another class. Where is the hole?

In my crotch haha.

Just keep your legs shut! You'll also stay out of trouble that way too!!!!!!! HAHAHA

-_- You can still do things with your legs shut. You'd know all about that momma

Shut it and go learn something useful!!!

* Low-key calling out your mother for giving blow jobs?

I met one of my neighbors. A 70 year old named John.

He was really nice.

Dating material??

Mom he is SEVENTY years old.

I know.

* When Mom is desperate for grandchildren AT ANY COST

MOTHER THURSDAY 10:58 AM

Why didn't you tell me Aunt Mildred was dead and in the ground already

Shit it was quick and I should have said something

We went to funeral only on Tuesday

* Whoops your aunt is dead sorry about that LOL

MOM JAN 18 3:38 PM

Hey so what's it like on extasy?

Bring me some soon

What?

Bring me some extasy

* MomDMA

MAMA   YESTERDAY 9:28 PM

U need to make n appointment with dr Bryan so u can get on birth control ok ?

Okay I'll give her a call do you have the number

Please make an appointment ASAP I don't want to be a grandmother 🐻

* Mom has no chill

MAMA   YESTERDAY 12:08 PM

Put Allison tablet and jacket in her backpack, we'll see if Emily will pick her up at the old house. She said she's done with work at 3:30, will you text her and ask her if she'll pick up Allison at the old house.

Did you get my text? Bring a couple cans of soda for yourself and your water if you want water. otherwise I have a half of sub for each of us, a banana for each of us, string cheese for each of us, and a little snicker bar for each of us

* She doesn't need to know every thought you've ever had

Are you coming home

I'm sick dying

Please bring orange juice and whatever else people drink when they're sick

No I'm not. Please go die in your room.

What's wrong with you?

Wow

I had to many saved screenshots to submit to the yourshittyfamily Instagram but I think this one takes it!

* Maternal instincts do not run in this family

MOM   **FRIDAY 2:25 PM**

????

Hi?

who is this

Brianna

???

Your daughter...

* Remember? The person who fell out of your vagina . . .

MAMA BEAR   TODAY 10:45 AM

Horrendous day so far. You ok?

Yeah just letting you know I got to work

I am SO hungover lol

TODAY 5:42 PM

What's for dinner?

Gin and tonic

PREACH 🙏

* Secret family recipe

MOM   WEDNESDAY 9:02 AM

Did you tell me your vagina is dry?

* If it wasn't before . . .

MOMMA   TODAY 5:56 PM

Have you talked to DAD?

He's driving me crazy

I have him in me 24/7.
Hard to take

ON ME LOL

Omg hahahahah

* Autocorrect ruins yet another life

MAMA BEAR　　　　　**WEDNESDAY 12:38 PM**

I really like my new gynecologist.
I think you would too.

* There are a few things you just don't want to share

MOM　　　　　**MAY 22 6:10 PM**

Haha

I said I wanted a puppy not a demon

* Look what I got you!

Mom—are you up?

Mom?

Mom—it's really important. I know it's late (or early) but I really need u right now.

Stevie—it's 2:30 a.m. . . . What's going on? Are you alright?

I just ate the most wonderful piece of reheated pizza.

....

You are demented.

* Nothing like being disappointed that your child isn't in imminent danger

MOM   FRIDAY 4:56 PM

I'm sorry about your butt honey. :/

* What does she know that he doesn't know?

MOMMY   TODAY 9:04 AM

:)

I organized the basement storage area last week

Wow! I'm jellO! I need to do that

You're jello? :P

Jealous, silly don't you know slang? I have to teach u everything?!

It's jelly, Mom!

* There's always room for Jell-O

MAMA   TODAY 4:54 PM

Hi MoFo!

😂 😂 😂 do you know what that means!?

More info please

Google mofo 😂 😂

* Nothing is more awkward than your
  mother calling you a motherfucker

MOM   OCT 16 12:44 PM

hey

WASSUP BIOTCH!!

That was so fetch

Are you watching mean girls?

Why are you so obsessed with me?

* Stop trying to make fetch happen

MOM   TUESDAY 12:47 PM

Hey there sweetie did you come by
while we were out of town?

Because we found Mexican
hats on the sofa 😑

* Adios, Mom

MOMMA   YESTERDAY 11:20 PM

I hate texting ahhhh. I'm not drunk.
I'm dicklexus lo. I miss your dad

Dicklexus????

* Dick Lexus, Private Investigator

MOM   JUL 12 4:09 PM

Do you have a pregnancy test at home?

Yeah   Lol

How many do you have? Should I wait
and try it when you're home?

I have one

You can have it

* This feels a little backward

MAMA   TODAY 8:52 AM

You are about to start your period.
You started February 16.

I know

You also have a week of pretty
bad pms beforehand

very true

A perfect storm

OMG

* THIS. ISN'T. HELPING!!!

MOMMA   TODAY 4:39 PM

Are you alive?

Nope

Ok good so I can save the tuition money

* Private schools are expensive

MUM   TUESDAY 9:48 AM

I just saw the most awesome cock a Range Rover with these awesome rooms and this black cock with white bottom Michelle that's my cock look it up

Oh my God I'm so sorry

I meant to say cock not cock SORRY!!!

Car**

* Autocockrect

MOM　　　　　　　　　　　THURSDAY 6:12 PM

Text me and let me know how it's going

THURSDAY 9:08 PM

Hewwwwooooo

Oh lort. I'm waiting. I'm going to take a shower and then u better tell me something

Oh hewwwwoooo what the heck.
U know I have ANXIETY......

Oh my. Pleeeeaaaassseeee just check in.

R u eloping??　　Geesh

I'm alive

Stop

I can't wait until you're a mother

* And she can't wait until she can put you in an old age home

MOM TODAY 10:34 AM

Dad did well and the surgery went as expected. He's in recovery and after he pees we get to go home. 👍

Bahaha!! Good!

* Please, more updates on Dad peeing

MOMMA BEAR TUESDAY 9:15 AM

What you and dad doing for vday

Dad and I are having non stop sex.

Thanks for the info

No problem

* BRB, gotta go kill myself

MOM   DEC 19 9:35 PM

All my lpve. Thank you for all your
advice.say hello to justin and remember
keep making love in the. Recommended.
Positions.i will pray everyday. Fo

r your uterus

* Do you have a Nigerian bank account you need help with?

MOM   SATURDAY 9:20 PM

What is playboy?

Mom u should be old enough to know this

You should be smart enough to find some friends

Speechless

* Mom doesn't need your backtalk

MOMMY   MAY 27 11:43 AM

What year were u born, 92 or 93

Wow mom

98!!!

* Apparently it wasn't a very memorable year

Any plans with the new guy up north?

I went up Friday and got home last night. It was freezing so outdoor activities were limited

I really don't want to know what kind of indoor activities you participated in.

MOM!!! Lord Jesus . . .

* Mostly just chess and blow jobs

Can I stay over at Zach's?

No

Why? Why don't u ever let me stay here? His mom is here

Fine. Dad and I will be having sex in your bed then tonight.

OMFG

* No, no, no! I'll come home!!!!!

Ty

Ty?

Thank you

Oh

That awkward moment when your mom knows more texting slang than you . . .

* FML

Your dad ate a dish rag and your dad had to pull it out of his butt today

Dog not dad

* I kind of wish it *was* Dad

FRIDAY 7:39 PM

I'm gonna become a stripper

That would be fine and dandy
if you could dance

Thanks mom

Yep!

* When your Mom doesn't believe in you

MOMMY

TODAY 7:04 AM

Happy birthday to you happy birthday to you
happy birthday my beautiful daughter Abbey
happy birthday to you!

love you, talk to you later! mom 🖤 💬 🎁

mom, you spelled my name wrong . . .

* Your name is whatever she says it is! She created you!

MOMMA

Why dont we arm wrestle for it

Cuz I don't have to. I'm the boss

Its cause your scared

Ya I don't want to see my 24 year old son
cry like a bitch

* Smackdown, courtesy of Mom

**Happy Birthday Mom!
Love you so much**

I love you too maybe

What?

* That whole unconditional love thing is bullshit

SH*TTY SIBLINGS

You grew up together. You shared a room. No one knows you better than your siblings. And no one knows them better than you. And they had better be careful or you'll tell everyone how fucking annoying they are.

BRODER JACKSON   **TODAY 9:08 PM**

What's the wifi here in Aspen

L1kmibuth0l3

Are you sure that's it?

No that says lick my butthole

OMG

I'VE LITERALLY BEEN TRYING
THAT FOR 20 MIN

* BEST. PRANK. EVER.

MADS

whatever

10:24 PM

Here...

I'm here!!!

Shut up bitch I'm trying to sleep

* It's 10:30 P.M. Who's the real bitch?

SISTAAAAA   MAR 3 2:08 AM

Hi sister I'm wasted

TODAY 12:33 AM

Hi sister I'm wasted

Hahahahaha

* Always great to catch up

88   YOUR SH*TTY FAMILY

STEVEN   **TODAY 3:53 PM**

You're an idiot
Happy birthday fuckboy

* It's nice to feel loved

BEN   **TODAY 3:10 PM**

Dad has done the biggest shit I've ever
seen and the toilet literally won't flush

No toilet paper, the actual shit won't go.
I've flushed it 3 times

And its still there full length, hasn't moved

LOL

Seriously LOL, mums gonna go mad

Send me a pic

* Too much information!!!

KEVIN MAR 16 3:43 PM

Omg my neighbor across the street pooped in his fucking garbage can!!!! I had to tell you

Haha how do you know???

I heard yelling, so I went outside

and he came out, put his ass over the side of the porch, and dropped a 5 dollar footlong in his garbage can

* Seems like a nice neighborhood

SUE SUNDAY 4:56 PM

Do you have a cd player & do u want a cd called The Main Event (john farnham, olivia newton, anthony warlow)?

is any of that a serious question?

* This might be the most serious question of all time

What should I eat for dessert?

Your butt

No really, what should I eat for dessert and please stop playing around

OK your balls

Eat YOUR butt

What should I eat for dessert and stuff that's not on my body

And stop saying that I was supposed to eat my balls for dessert

* But have you ever *tried* eating your balls?

Becca had her baby

I didn't know she was pregnant

She's your sister...

* Close-knit family

GARY   THURSDAY 1:28 PM

I think you broke my radio in my truck.

How???

What could I have possibly done to it? I bet it has to do with you jumping the battery

No. It was making noise I never heard the radio make.

Sounded like Rap Music.

* HiGARYous

KELSEY   OCT 28 3:28 PM

Do people ever confuse your seizures for you trying to twerk?

All the time.

* She's just tryna' shake what her mama gave her

MOLLY   TODAY 9:16 PM

You got a date tonight?

Nope I just got done babysitting

That's good, but all money and no date means you gotta buy your own dinner!

Haha that's always the case

You need to find a rich guy and quick, because it's all about the money $$$$$

* Nothing like a sister who really believes in you

TONY   FRIDAY 2:43 PM

I just farted so hard I scared the rabbit

Seriously?

* To be fair, rabbits scare easily

Why is there a stain on my back seat?!

It's not what u think it is don't worry I put the left over spaghetti back there and it opened up and got sauce on ur seat so I tried scrubbing it.

I thought I cleaned it good

Is that why it smells like Clorox?!

I used the 409. Is that not good to use?

Cuz I figured marinara sauce stains so I tried getting it with water first and then used the 409

Hopefully it doesn't ruin my interior

Well I ate some of the leftover spaghetti and it ruined MY interior if you know what I mean

* Hahahahahahahahahahahahahahahahahahahahahaha

LUCKY   **DEC 12 8:13 AM**

Whatcha doing?

Pooping

So am I

Now I'm going to shower

OK. I'm still pooping

* What is this family eating?

KRISTY   **FRIDAY 10:39 AM**

Is everything OK?

No. We decided it's dandruff not lice

Still gross

* Take a bath you goddamn savages

TIM   YESTERDAY 2:54 PM

Going on a date tonight. Mtg him right after work at east sides. Kinda nervous.

Go poo before you leave work.

Hahahaahhaaah omg.

* Actually *very* good advice

JEN   WEDNESDAY 7:46 AM

Fuuuuuuuuuuuuck

I had a dream that I gave a hand job to a guy with an uncircumsized wiener ahahahahahahahaha lmao lmao wtffff

Wtf

I don't know who the guy was!

* I had a dream

CHARLES   YESTERDAY 9:30 PM

U good?

YESTERDAY 10:38 PM

Hello Ans me plz

I need to know u r ok

Fucking call me

Bitch

Psycho

* The stalker vibe is strong in this family

SARAH　　　　　　　　　　　**JAN 19 10:19 AM**

Remember "You don't have to be
lonely are farmersonly.com"
Good commercial!

* You're probably going to be single forever

SUEZ　　　　　　　　　　　**FRIDAY 2:40 PM**

Came home and found this.
Look closely . . . Dead? Asleep?

Hibernating.

* *National Geographic* has nothing on this hibernation joke

EDDIE TUESDAY 9:04 AM

What blood is bad when you shit?

Dark. Why??

Okay. I have bright red but I get it all the time.

Why? are you having too much anal sex?

Lmao no just shitting to much

* Please hold me, I'm scared

SIS TODAY 11:24 AM

Happy birthday fat ass!!! 🍑

Thanks nasty hoe

* #love

TOBY

I'm not trying to be an alarmist but both of you should store extra water, canned meats, canned food items, a hand held can opener, butane lighter, battery powered lanterns, matches, and cash in your apartment.

Buy a gun if you can and don't tell anyone. Something could happen this month if you are paying attention to the news and understand prophecy. 😀

* When your brother is a doomsday prepper

AGNES SATURDAY 2:41 PM

U alive?

Ya just hungover

Light weight

* Called out by your own sister :/

DAVE WEDNESDAY 4:35 PM

Do you have a gun I can borrow?

For what?

* It's personal

WILLIAM TUESDAY 7:26 AM

any good news?

I won five bucks on a scratch ticket, didn't get stuck behind the train on my way to work and I get the keys to my condo in less than a week

cool. I had a regular bowel movement 🚽 👀

high five

lol.

* Nothing like a supportive family!

JO JO   APRIL 22 3:34 PM

Is your bum covered in bleach now?

Nope :)

Too bad

You could use a nice ass hole bleach

Wow

* Sister knows best

MATT   TODAY 10:37 AM

Feeling any better today?

TODAY 12:41 PM

Ya bish. Hit that sizzurp

* That awkward moment when you realize your bro is Lil' Wayne

ANNE FEB 4 11:05 AM

Good Facebook picture. Your eyes look puffy. You ok? Trying to get sick?

* So you're saying he looks good?

JENNIFER TODAY 10:29 AM

Dog food lid backwards is dildo of God

TODAY 12:04 PM

I can't even 😂

* ALL HAIL DILDO OF GOD

JESSICA TODAY 8:10 PM

I need help

With? I'm watching twilight w dad lol

* She's sorry if you're being kidnapped, but she's Team Jacob

ELEANOR

Hi did you feel alright after last night's dinner?

Yes. R u not well?

Yeah I'm actually sick today

Maybe karma?

* Karma, like your sister, is a bitch

EMMA

It's COCKtober 🍆 🐔 u know what that means •• 👅 Dick sucking awareness month 😱 🌀 🐻 send this to 12 of ur closest hoes 🐷 that love that dick 🍆🍆🍆 💦💦💦

wth... seriously. That is terrible. You sound like a whore.

* This is just another holiday . . .

SOPHIE   THURSDAY 11:10 AM

I like my sweater you got me with the
scarf. I'm about to wear it dildo shopping
with the girls from work.

I'm glad you like it

* It's important to have a good dildo-shopping scarf

LAURA NOV 13 3:48 PM

Open the gate I have to poo real bad . . .
Nearly there 💩

💩

Already open

I have some friends over

Btw

ohhhhh 😳

💩

* Literally Your Shitty Family

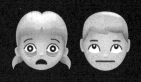

OLD PEOPLE SAY THE DARNDEST THINGS

They're so old and so cute. They come from a time when telegraphs were a thing and so was polio. But now they have phones and all the time in the world to bother you.

GRANPAPA

OCT 17 10:42 PM

love you

Young people can die

* Love you too?

GRANDMA   AUG 14 10:59 AM

> Munchkin you are rapidly falling
> from number 1. I haven't heard
> from you for ages. I miss you!
> Not good 🖤 🖤

* This grandma bizarrely writes exactly like Donald Trump tweets

MEEMAW   TODAY 3:59 PM

> Happy birthday 🎂

> Thank you grandma!!

> Your f ing welcome

* Savage!

GRANNY   FEB 11 2:38 PM

> Come by help me with email. Love u, Grandma

* Most grandma text of all time

Well Chance is biting his own dick, which sounds awful but he's really just biting til he's hard and then moaning and then he stops.

Was just wondering if that was a sign of maybe an infection although nothing's red or swollen or anything??

He's masturbating.

. . .

* Who wants to go visit Grandma?

Angel swallowed the foot she chewed off her stuffed fuck toy . . .

Uh what?

* Does she mean she fucked off the foot of her chew toy?

GRANDMA CELL   YESTERDAY 7:18 AM

Happy Birthday Frankie. Hope you have a great
21st day. Please make it a sober one. Love Gram

* Zero percent chance

GRAN   FEB 24 2:20 PM

You've gotten your butt hole
bleached

No

You should it the new thing

Why????

So it's not brown idk scratch it off
the bucket list

Cause it's the thing to do

* Anal Bleaching Tips from Grandma, 100/100

Ok got half balls for grandpa

What?

Goofball

What?

Okay I little freaky ball you heat on grass with a stick

What the hell does that even mean???

Golf

⭑ OMG. I CAN'T. STOP. JUST STOP. PLEASE STOP.

Ha ha just learned to use these...

Oh great now I can expect to get emoji icons from you all the time?

Stop it! You can't communicate only with emojis!!!!

💗💗💗💗

Use your words

Uuugh

* No one could read Grandma's will because it was all in emoji

PAWPAW YESTERDAY 7:52 AM

Why are you up?

Work. Why are you up?

Taking your grandma to radiation.

I now use her left breast as a night light.

* Too soon?

GRANDPA FRIDAY 11:52 AM

Hey do u have more baby pictures of me?

Like baby baby pictures

FRIDAY 1:13 PM

The doctors said to wait to take
pictures until your skull reached
a normal state for humans

* Unfortunately that still hasn't happened

GRANDMA SUNDAY 8:19 PM

Have you ever seen people that are smoking those things that are not cigarettes?

Not the ones that are smoking pot

That is called vaping.

* Vaping for grandmas

GRANDMA JOANN JAN 14 9:58 AM

Who is all going to cancun

just Travis and I

Really. Well sounds like a good place to get that d...............

What??

* She's not wrong

I'm playing Cards Against Humanity. Quite fun.

Oh god.

What's a glory hole?

Grandma no. Just no.

* BACK AWAY FROM THE GAME

TODAY 9:43 AM

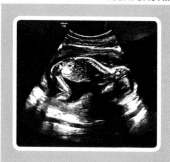

**Meet your first
great grandchild**

TODAY 11:17 AM

I am making pie crust now

Okay

* Nobody cares about your baby

GRAMS   FRIDAY 6:37 PM

Do u have a wine stopper?

No I usually drink the whole bottle when I open it 🍷 🍷 🍷

* Your grandma can teach you a lot

POP POP   TUESDAY 8:14 AM

What is your birthdate?

04/26/1988

Weren't you there?

Nope.

That was your grandma's husband

* Rough way to find out you're not actually related

GRANDMA   MAR 16 8:30 PM

> Happy birthday grandma!! Hope you had a
> wonderful day. Can't wait for the wedding.
> Love you so much!! —Jess :)

I'm not ur grandma. this is the
wrong number sorry

* Honestly, she's probably just tired of you texting her

GRAN   FEB 19 10:22 AM

I tried to email you a news story
about toxic shock.

Did you receive it?

> No lol but why did you send me that?

Interesting story and to make sure that
you change tampons frequently

* Please keep your thoughts out of your granddaughter's vagina

I just wanted to ask wat does (wym) stand for?

What do you mean?

I'm asking what wym means.

I know. "WHAT DO YOU MEAN"

I was texting your cousin Max and that's what he put.

It means What Do You Mean

What?

* It means what do you mean

I just finished my grad school applications. Woo-hoo!

D
A
Yea!! Congestion s

You should probably just start over with that text

Congratulations
Yea!!

There ya go

Thanks :)

* Slow it down. Start at the beginning. Good boy

POP   JUN 14 12:49 AM

I smoked a hit

Tight

Yea tight.

* Please stop trying to be cool, Grandpa. No one "smokes a hit"

GRAN   TODAY 7:35 AM

Hey! You called me by accident I think!

It was accident sorry.

Haha that's ok I just thought you loved me for once

Nope. Accident.

* She won't make that mistake again

GRAMPS   JUL 23 10:50 PM

Quick question . . . have you ever
been on tinder?

* Swipe left

GPA   TODAY 12:31 AM

You can't say happiness without saying penis!

* Wise words from any grandfather!

GMAMA   YESTERDAY 11:43 PM

Love you. Stay independent...get your
education and career. Never rely on a
man.. look for a true equal

As long as they eat your ass like a cupcake

go to bed.

* First things first

GRANDPAPPY   TUESDAY 3:54 PM

hope your looking after yourself X

Nah all the drugs and prostitutes
are taking their toll.

No money left for food.
All me teeth have fallen out.

* He's a real charmer, and a pirate to boot

GRAN   APR 12 7:15 PM

Something's wrong with my iPad. I've been
trying to watch the last episode all day

Try to restart the whole thing. Press the top
button and the main one until you see an apple

I guess I used up all our wifi 😔

* Yeah, that's probably what happened

GRANDPA   TODAY 9:17 AM

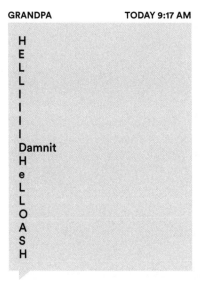

H
E
L
L
I
I
I
I
Damnit
H
e
L
L
O
A
S
H

* You need a new hobby, Grandpa

GRAN PAPA   TODAY 11:08 PM

Yo bitch kitty, hope you're feeling better.

thanks

* Grandpas aren't quite as soft and caring
as Grandmas when you're sick

GRANDMA   MONDAY 3:43 PM

What is this? 🌽

Corn?

Looks like 3 penises

I didn't know penises were green

When they're not ripe

* 🌽 🌽 🌽 We do not recommend having sex with this

GRAN   JUN 12 4:26 PM

You should date Evan Spiegel

Wtf

Who is that

He is hot

Wtf

He is 25 and his net worth is $2.1 billion

You don't know who he is?

Idiot

Omg gran

* Any other billionaires you think I should date?

I'm on the plane now. I'll talk to ya later

Ok have a great trip

All of the computers crashed so I'm stuck on this plane now. Might miss my connecting flight

Oh fish cake

Fish cake?

Nice way of saying oh FUCK

* Go fish cake yourself

Hey do u know what blue waffle is?

* Don't Google don't Google don't Google don't Google . . .

GRANDPA

where u b at?

1:17 AM

where u b at?

1:31 AM

is anybody out there?

* He's not responding until you learn to talk like an adult

THE DREADED GROUPCHAT

The only thing worse than a text from one of your family members is a text from all of your family members.

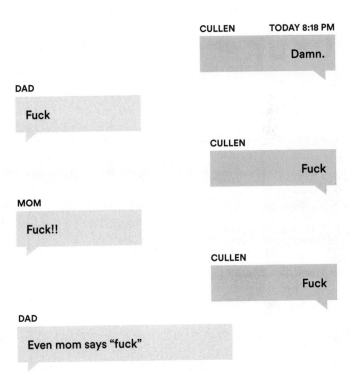

* Family bonding time

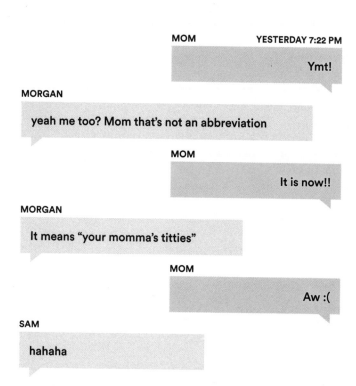

MOM YESTERDAY 7:22 PM

Ymt!

MORGAN

yeah me too? Mom that's not an abbreviation

MOM

It is now!!

MORGAN

It means "your momma's titties"

MOM

Aw :(

SAM

hahaha

* This went south quickly!

ABIGAIL　　　　　　　　　　　　　　　　　　　FEB 3 2:18 PM

Hey can you guys describe me in one sentence? It's for a job interview

Approachable yet authoritative

ELIZABETH

Fun when drunk

MOM

Good leader

ELIZABETH

Formerly nose-pierced

DAD

Skilled at engaging in repetitive alcohol consumption behind the back of authority figures while maintaining a goody two-shoes persona at all times

ABIGAIL

This was a mistake.

* Left the door wide open on this one . . .

MOM APR 3 10:17 PM

Good night all..

DAD

I don't care. . . .

EVAN

😭 Real nice. . .

MOM

Way to make me feel loved . . . . . .

* Divorce papers will arrive in the morning

MOMMA

OCT 12 2:11 PM

Booked up a cruise.
We r going to the Bahamas

JULIE

Yayyy :)

RYAN

will there be wifi?

JULIE

you're an ungrateful piece of shit?...

* Only concerned with the bare necessities

PAPA   **MAR 2 1:26 PM**

> Once your mum got sick on vacation and I had to carry her. TOO HEAVY!

MUM

> Oh that's choice you fat fuck

PAPA

> How dare you speak to your father like that you little rat turd

SISSY

> MUM SAID THAT NOT ME

PAPA

> Your still a rat turd

MUM

> No zip line in the world is going to carry your fat ass without pulling down a forest

* Your family is always there to make you feel like shit about yourself

MOM

So, I saw a blurb on tv this a.m. Texting 'K' is now rude and means 'I'm done with you, stop texting me?'

SARAH

K

JAMES

K

REBECCA

K

JOSH

K

NANCY

I'm done with you stop texting me

* Lesson learned

DAD DEC 20 11:11 AM

Do you all want bras from Victoria Secret, and what size are you?

RACHEL

???

LINDSEY

Ew.

* I think I'd rather be dead . . . and 34C

MOM

To whomever is eating the cookie dough: STOP, you're more than welcome to make cookies. Seriously STOP!!!!!!!

JULIE

I love cookies

SISTER

* Use your words

MARGOT   TODAY 7:18 AM

Happy Birthday Mom !!!!

MOM

Thank you. You're first and you didn't forget.

MARGOT

Love you let me know if you get called.

MATT   8:16 AM

Happy birthday mom. Love you.

MOM

Thanks, Matt. Margot beat you this year.

* It's good to only love one child at a time

WHO'S THE PARENT NOW?

Your parents are definitely older than you, but that doesn't necessarily make them more mature.

Were r u

Can I hav an oreo

* So Oreo. Much Dad

MOM CELL   **FRIDAY 9:44 PM**

I learned a new word tonight

Do I even want to know?

Humane

No

Bulk ale

No

Bukkake

* Please don't learn any more new words!

Is everything good?

Fuck you

Did u go cliff diving yet?

Yeah we went today

* Did Mom just get body-snatched for a second?

Hahaha so what happened at children's hospital that you don't work there now?

Not sure maybe I failed drug test

...what?

* D.A.R.E.

MOTHER   FRIDAY 4:09 PM

I got an owi lol

I mean an owwwi. I smashed my thumb
in my car door this morn :(

* You're giving my brain an owwwi

DADDY   NOV 24 8:29 PM

Are you there? I need a lift home I'm drumk

what time you going home? I at the yacht club

* Sorry, Dad. It's time you learn a lesson about responsibility

DADDY   THURSDAY 6:32 PM

Your mother ate goldfish edibles.
Too many, she got sick 😵

* Once you pop, you can't stop

MOMMA

The girls asked if I wanted to go hot boxing tonight... I'm so excited to go. cant wait!

7:46 PM

Ok. Be safe. If you get the munchies I ordered Thai food for dinner.

* Umm. Are you sure you know what that means?

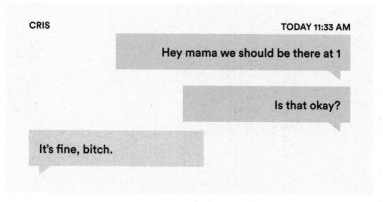

CRIS

Hey mama we should be there at 1

Is that okay?

It's fine, bitch.

* Speak your feelings

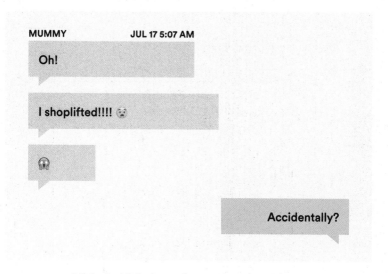

MUMMY   JUL 17 5:07 AM

Oh!

I shoplifted!!!! 😢

😱

Accidentally?

* I don't think she understands the meaning
  of the word "accidentally"

DAD   **MONDAY 11:55 AM**

Tank ass

Tank ass

FRIDAY 6:17 PM

U suck

FRIDAY 8:18 PM

U suck

Bitch

* Tank ass

DAD   YESTERDAY 7:18 PM

In other news I've just given birth
to the biggest turd 💩

🙀 🙀 That is foul.

That's kinda what my face looked like too!

Have you been on the toilet this
whole convo??!

Obvs.

* He's been naked the whole time you've been talking

It is time now for the acknowledgments.

This is the place where I, the person with the book, will thank the people who made the book into the book.

This is a book about family and first I must thank the people who were the family to the book. Bill Dixon put long and fun hours into making this book funny and good and nice. Heather and Aron and Peter and Matthew watched the whole thing grow and nurtured it and me through its adolescence.

The book also has a biological family. Samantha Weiner is the godmother of the book and she and Devin and Heesang and all the people at Abrams who believed in the book. Jess Regel and all the people at Foundry made the book actually happen. Christina Kuo and all the people at CAA and David Fox and Jessica Bergman and all the other wonderful people who made sure this book had a skeleton and a spine and blood and meat and tasty wings. I also must thank my TV family for laughing with me always, even when my face looked angry or confused. I also must thank my accountant Tim, whom I have never met.

Tamar and Tal and Shir and Dubi and Robert and Gingi and Murphy and Bunny and the three dead frogs who taught me about my own mortality at a young age. Molly and Piper and Pikachu and the strange violent animal that if I ever find I will kill but I am also glad it exists because it taught us to be strong and to believe in others. Pete and Cassie and Georgia and Nyah and Nicole and Bernerrd.

Look, it's a lot of fucking people. There are a lot of people involved in doing everything. I probably forgot some people, but I'm not perfect, get off my fucking back.

But more than anything, I need to thank you, the reader, and the Instagram followers, because together we have fun and smile and enjoy four or five seconds of every day together. If you add that all up, at the end of this, we all kind of know each other pretty well. So, you're family too. We're all a little family. And your family is what you make it. Thanks to all the people who make themselves family to other people.

Thanks to everyone. Except for my neighbor Gary who I hope chokes on a sandwich and dies.

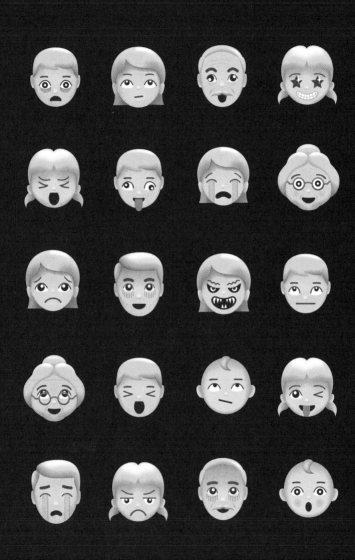

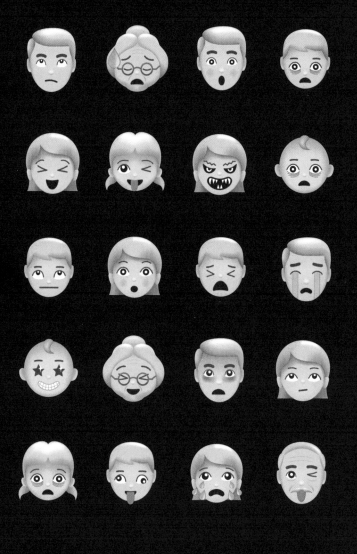